GOODBYE, BABY

GOODBYE, BABY

by
Gaylord Brewer

Accents Publishing • Lexington, Kentucky • 2026

Printed in the United States of America

Accents Publishing
Editor: Katerina Stoykova
Cover Image: *Meandering Landscape with River* by Piet Mondrian, 1906–1907

Library of Congress Control Number: 2026932336
ISBN: 978-1-961127-21-0
First Edition

Accents Publishing is an independent press for brilliant voices. For a catalog of current and upcoming titles, please visit us on the Web at

www.accents-publishing.com

CONTENTS

If today was not a crooked highway
If tonight was not a crooked trail
If tomorrow wasn't such a long time
Then lonesome would mean nothing to you at all

—Dylan

2008 – 2024

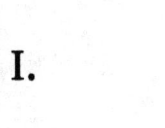

I.

Blood and flesh and salt—proportioned
by temperament or as you were taught.
Add to these whatever remains,
forgotten bits and scraps often discarded.
Only fire, the essential last element.
Braise, roast, simmer, sear? Ideology
doesn't matter. The season doesn't matter.
Blood, flesh, salt, flame. Tattoo these
in memory. Seconds, decades, eternity.
Candle, bowed head, night at the door.
An invocation of silence. Your dish served
at table where once they all gathered.

The scars on the leather of my hands,
my arms, my face, trails of a wayward map,
promise of fool's gold for a life spent.
Fool, indeed. Forgive me. My back argues
every one of fifty-nine years
and murders thought. In the sky, clouds
blunt the heat that has slaughtered us.
I move ponderously, hose in hand—
caladium, coreopsis, finca, cactus orchid,
hosta, thyme and sage, rosemary, basil,
hibiscus, coxcomb, coleus, all in half-hearted
acceptance. Every day, Lucy more frail.

We park at the bank, proceed to our Saturday vendors.
A small lemon cake, two dressed trout "swimming yesterday."
The hippie couple who supplies our lettuces away at a wedding
so we console with zucchini, risk some early tomatoes.
I sound a watermelon and hoist the sack to my shoulder.
Oyster mushrooms, a greasy carton of the garlic scape pesto.
Good peaches rare as precious stones. I hand an Asian child
a tenner and she bags six fruits. The costs, staggering.
The 100°F morning, staggering. I'm light-headed, a bit crazed.
By the time our costly bounty's stowed, that hopeless
shallow-breathed panic is coming on—I need to see Lucy,
see her *now*, head hard for the house to get there in time.

My old dog naps at my feet, wheezing quietly,
while in the adjoining room my wife bathes.
We have achieved another Sunday afternoon,
no visitors, no complicit or unnecessary words.
Bird-cry, wind-whisper. Every sworn promise
to myself I have failed again. Lucy at 22 pounds.
I carry her outside to her business, hip bones
prominent beneath that plush white coat.
Arid heat molests us into further submission,
a faded butterfly lands on my shoulder although
I doubt it mistakes me for Master Whitman.
Out here in reality, the garden fights for its life.

ℛ

Strive to not be a tragic idiot. What will come,
will come. After the blaze of the Slaughter Pen,
where Negley pulled his surviving boys
from Sheridan's trap, the path turns toward
a relief of mottled shade, nary a ghost in sight.
No human either, just you, the suspicious robins,
cool greenery beneath a dome of carnage.
Nearby, the boot of your car heavy with clams,
mussels, red shrimp, Dungeness crab legs on ice,
two bottles of gin for your next rebirth.
Don't be an idiot. Enjoy your battlefield stroll.
Chat with the dead all you like. Then go home.

I searched back and forth through the pages,
forth, back, for the quote I'd read night before
concerning humans as the only creatures
who destroy the present lamenting the future.
Stated better. A short book. I was certain
I'd find the lines easily. Then I began to doubt
the name of the author, whether this was
the correct text, whether the words existed.
This heat's made us mad, torpid, insensible.
I take in the trash, a young fellow stumbles past—
a zombie. At the creek, two flushed does,
a juvenile heron, hardly bother to fear me.

No more of this softness. This kowtowing
to comfort. I'm going native—limestone ledges
for defense, last thicket of woods for refuge.
Suture my own wounds, write verses
with the needle dipped in an ink of blood.
That sort of thing. The Rambo/Rimbaud duality
I've waited a pampered lifetime to embrace.
When the young Maasai warrior struggled
to build fire without matches, some wag offered
his Bic lighter. You want a season in Hell?
The punji pit to sharpen your resolve?
Come on in. Just don't forget the body bags.

✺

Twelve filth-streaked eggs, never to be born,
snug in their crate. Twelve desirous creatures
of the Zodiac. Twelve notches in the clockface.
Vagary of midnight, uncertainty of noon.
Twelve tortured lines of the forlorn ghazal.
Twelve ribs each side of the human cage,
awaiting the first blow. Twelve walking the moon,
twelve royalty in the deck. Twelfth Night
before Epiphany. Twelfth Station of the Cross
and twelve betrayed apostles. Twelve-gauge broken
beneath the bed. Twelve months from here to
our wilderness. Twelve lies of self-belief.

We submitted to the sovereignty of our chaos.
Came to believe in a lesser Power than ourselves.
Gave our lives to the Darkness as we understood It.
Made a prideful and selective moral inventory.
Admitted all to Darkness, ourselves, and no other.
Readied for Darkness to further embolden us.
Entreated It to remove our hesitancy.
Listed those we had harmed and renounced apology.
Made amends to none, except to further injure.
Continued our mastery and confessed to nothing.
As understood, vowed to better comprehend It.
Awakened, carried these principles forever forward.

July 4th, but I remain King as I shuffle in Royal
Slippers, issue a decree or two to a silent Queen.
When I command my dog to lick the Royal Hand,
she opens one lazy eye to her Majesty.
In the courtyard, I distribute bread and water
to a thankless rabble of robin and squirrel. Tonight's
brief display of might—*feux d'artifice* as the impudent
French have it—Jack missile, Roman candle,
rocket launched from a bottle of good Bordeaux.
Bring me drink!, I bellow to the empty hall. It's good
to be King, though at times I wonder if, without
a single musket fired, the revolution's already over.

❧

With whatever bullshit eminent domain, and little
resistance, the airport bought, razed, cleared it all.
Highland Park—sprawl of lower-middle-class blocks,
narrow alleys, cracked sidewalks. My grandmothers
lived in modest houses, great-great aunt Grace
even after Pirtle died, Pirtle's brother King, wife Nell.
My parents escaped. The roots remained,
and I spent many childhood hours roaming there.
Years later, I drove through lush grasses crisscrossed
by a grid of abandoned streets, eerily beautiful.
Everyone's long dead. The airport never expanded,
and decades-on I suppose those ghostly fields remain.

Blue grosbeak pecking at parched grass
beside a baking creek bed. Willow flycatcher—
I kid you not—on a neighbor's fencepost.
Two hours earlier, beyond this very window,
blue-gray gnatcatcher, arcing striped tail,
plucking string that guides the morning glory.
A heady day for geeks like us, topped off
moments ago by baby gray tree frog smaller
than a pinky nail, pointed face, pale as dust,
snoozing in scarlet-edged bowl of coxcomb leaf
in the whiskey barrel by the redbud sapling.
Here: This map I've drawn to guide you.

I have deadheaded the season's final lilies,
filled feeder and bath, hugged wife and dog
and spoke quietly to both, printed the route
to a stranger's home where tonight I'll attempt sleep.
Now, just the car pointed north, the coming hours.
Now just to keep moving and head empty,
calmly fulfill the obligations at hand.
This afternoon, my frail mother dozing in her chair,
mouth ajar, television blasting. I've telephoned
twice that I'm coming, but my arrival at the door,
once registered, will be a huge surprise.
Room #131. Code for the exit hall 5309*.

Then I am home, Lucy alive, I'm loving on her,
kissing Claudia, I'm home! Somewhere
near Dinosaur World and Guntown Mountain
the engine warning light flickered out, I felt
rumblings of a heady foolish hope, floored it.
Raced through seven minutes of storm,
emerged to blue sky, then my favorite stretch
of highway on earth, 266 South, and I swear that,
careering 22.4 miles through Adams Grove,
Norene, across the Rutherford County line
flat-out toward Lascassas where the road ends,
I was out of body, out of my mind, I was flying!

Dear Marshall Crenshaw: Would you remember
Bluebird Café "in the round" from thirty years ago?
We'd come to hear Bill Morrissey, were stunned
by a raging fellow named Malcolm Holcombe.
You and David Olney, and an evening for the ages.
Bill died in 2011, age 59, alone in a hotel room
days after a house concert with nine in attendance.
Olney died on stage in 2020, mid-song, age 71.
Stopped, said "I'm sorry," never opened eyes again.
Malcolm, age 68, died four months ago of cancer.
I was listening yesterday to his posthumous album,
when I thought of you, age 70. Hope you're well.

On this day, July 11th, Aaron Burr slayed
Alexander Hamilton in duel, Skylab crashed
to earth, *To Kill a Mockingbird* was published,
Pope Clement VII excommunicated Henry VIII
for his marriage to Anne Boleyn, and poet
Gaylord Brewer, nearing the end of his career,
as he approached the creek that brutally
hot afternoon, heard at once the fluid warble
of the tanager, then high in the shaded canopy
of sycamore and birch spied her, the elusive female,
lovely olive-green plumage, flitting branch
to branch, in song as if for an audience of one.

The broken earth hard as stone. Each regretted
step a jolt up the leg, to the spine. My unconceived
children crowd the door, pale arms extended
in one more grab. I never cared, they chatter—
now it's their turn. What of the unborn grandchild,
light of my last days? I tell'm to get lost, go to Hell,
go to the library of tedious souls and read their reviews.
Just go. At 5:47 a.m. I peered out the front window:
robins, cardinals, rabbit noshing brittle grass,
on cue a single doe, lean but beautiful, strolling
the perimeter. Not yet too hot to move, to think,
to live, the world proceeding as well without me.

❧

That summer in Spain, beneath Monserrat
and the Black Virgin, *La Moreneta*, that summer
Ghost first appeared across a stone bridge
in the village, I began to sculpt the small heads.
Empty eyes, distended foreheads, twisted
mouth holes. A nail through temple or jowl,
the wound of the scream sutured with twigs.
What did Ghost want from me? I stretched clay
by hand, each blind howling skull. When I left
that life with a lie to return, I wrapped the heads
in cloth, buried the most tortured in my bag.
Some survived, lasted years before dissolving.

II.

Lumbering hedgehog, doe clattering over stone.
How can I blame them for fleeing? Still, the world
can surprise you. Yellow-crowned night heron
raises an orange foot slowly from the muck. It stops,
turns in silhouette, inquires with a luminous eye.
Yards away, white-spotted fawn, ears enormous,
watching. I am still now, conscious of my breath.
Three old toms, gray heads, long trembling wattles,
shake themselves awake in the shade, begin to preen.
Just like that our tableau complete. We continue
to wait, quietly alive together in this flash of eternity.
The weight of the waning day begins to lift.

I often keep an eye on who passed at my age, potential
peeps forever, this year 59ers who failed at big 6-0.
Gypsy Rose Lee, William the Conqueror, Rock Hudson,
Rabelais, Ovid, Erasmus, Virginia Woolf, Bill Bixby.
On and on at their lavish digs in oblivion: Dostoevsky,
Coolio, Clare of Assisi, Sitting Bull. Solomon, Peckinpah,
Dred Scott, Jezebel. Peter Lorre, Conway Twitty. I'd aspire
to hang with the hippest: Cassavetes, Cromwell, Capote,
Sher Shar Suri (1st sultan of Suri), Madame Blavatsky,
Fanny Brice … Good crowd to die with. And Clark Gable,
the King, awaiting the birth of his first child when
the second heart attack sent him crashing to the party.

Even in its sorry state after two months of drought,
what would we had done without the creek
this summer of our anger, fear, our anticipated grief
itself already a preemptive grieving? My wife goes early,
Lucy and I asleep in cage and bed, before the day
catches fire. I take my insensible turn in late afternoon.
Today six big tom turkeys, bad boys with lots of pluck
who high-step aside only once I'm among them.
Out of the algae-choked water, over stones of the dry
cascade, a single mink, wet and dark. My wife reported
it a week ago. I had no reason to doubt her, but
these sad days as they are, I needed to see to believe.

Cynan, how may I thank you? Two calves birthed dead,
disfigured in blood, a pitiless drought, what's left of
the man's hand after the tractor, his wife's scarred wrists.
In 117 spare pages of a single day, you've distracted me
from my woes. The trusting canine, joyous to live
despite tumor and festering wound, injected by the vet
and none but the daughter Emma to witness. Emma in turn
will be dead in eleven days, after the poison mushroom
opened like an angel. I've alternated your chapters
with Jim's suicide letters to Yesenin, his paeans to the rope.
You guys should share notes, somewhere other than
in my head. Paint the town. Our raucous last night together.

I park at Bradley's Creek Baptist by the cemetery,
hike north over the old bridge, east on Oregan
where it plateaus, curves toward a blue ring of hills.
I've a phone in my pocket for emergencies re Lucy.
Clouds offer a promise we are desperate to believe.
As I return, a big Angus dairy cow, heavy with milk,
watching me, begins to urinate, non-stop torrent,
on and on, her frothing miction pooling beneath her.
I roust seven noisy killdeer, five in the sheep field.
My hour up, I drive the long way round. Two handsome
bucks cross Twelve Corners, a sheen of water glazes
the windshield. That is everything I can tell you.

After a suddenly former friend's clumsy and failed
lunge at my jewels—news to me—he tipsily explained
that he loved eating pussy, why not sucking cock?
I repeated this peerless logic to another friend,
who responded on cue: So that's like, I love scallops,
why wouldn't I love swordfish? The old gourmand's
dead now, out-of-mind dementia those final months
when he wouldn't have known a dick from applesauce.
His last word, reported by his daughter, "fuck'm,"
laudable if a bit sweeping. Myself, I adore scallops,
with that proper sear that's so elusive. Or raw, thinly
sliced, pinch of Camargue salt, otherwise undressed.

We soaked our sandals when crossing the Rubicon.
They dried out quick enough on that dusty road
to Damascus. We marched on, parched for epiphany,
a "name-changer" to cement places in cruel history,
define us as the good guys we believed ourselves.
Late in the story for resurrections, ours didn't happen.
Donkey this, leper that, never the cool cleansing sip
of water. The dead stagger from tombs, consider,
retreat behind their stone. It's all about image. Crushed
rebellion was bad for ours. You know how this ends.
I just pray, 6,000 bemused, severed heads lining
the Appian Way, mine looks handsome on its pike.

The bagworm suspended in cocoon of twigs,
hauling its weight upward by a single silk.
What does it seek, mid-air and vulnerable?
As suddenly as the green June beetles appear,
brushy black antennae, iridescent scarab shells,
hurtling low over the grasses, they vanish.
Unmoving in turbid water, a sunfish's muted
colors. The woman opens her grief journal
to begin: "Today was today, each hour an hour
passed. The sky was the sky as it darkened.
Every moment, I must remind myself *that* life
is over. Remind myself he will not return."

The costly tomatoes and peppers, onions and garlic
of the gazpacho, watermelon, arugula, sheep's feta
of the salad, all from farmers at our Saturday market.
Whole trout, harvested and dressed hours before,
stuffed with thyme from our garden. Sweet peaches
for dessert from the old man we like. We, good citizens
of summer, good neighbors, fair and conscientious
eaters. Though honestly, arugula, out of season, bought
at a big box grocer. Truth told, the lemon too a lie,
the virgin oil, the wine. The rest can be trusted,
mostly. A rich July meal. Oh, and the gin and olive.
The gin always a problem. Or solution, depending.

I am Aries, my wife Libra, so when the horoscope
assures she will lure me "as Stendahl," why not worry?
Referring I assume to Stendahl Syndrome—hallucination,
fainting before great beauty. Will my "fierce confidence,"
"hunger for action" defend? A matter of Fire (me)
versus Air (her)? Our cutie dog also a Libra,
complicating my situation. Psychologists debate whether
Stendahl Syndrome even exists, though nurses at Florence's
Santa Maria Nuova Hospital report tourists dizzy
and disoriented after approaching Michelangelo's *David*.
In 2018, also in the Uffizi, a man suffered a heart attack
gazing at Botticelli's *The Birth of Venus*. He survived.

No more reprieve,
no miracles.
It has arrived.
My beautiful girl.
Here—your
twelve lousy lines.
Now please
just let us be
in these last days.
My baby's in pain.
Lucy leaving us.
Lucy dying.

❧

Brumous: *adj.*, of gray skies or fog; relating to winter, sunlessness.

Abditory: *n.*, secret refuge; hiding place to preserve most-valued things.

Abluvion: *n.*, that which has been washed away.

Balter: *vb.*, to dance artlessly, clumsily, but with enjoyment.

Redamancy: *n.*, act of loving one who loves you; a love returned in full.

Tacenda: *n.*, what is better unsaid, acknowledged in silence.

Objets trouvés: *n.*, objects past their use, their beauty discovered again.

Eidetic: *adj.*, (psychology) denoting images with unusual vividness.

Cortege: *n.*, solemn procession, esp. for funeral; entourage, retinue.

Nemophilist: *n.*, haunter of the woods; lover of the forest's solitude.

Offing: *n.*, distant stretch of ocean visible from land; foreseeable future.

Psithurism: *n.*, the sound of wind through trees.

❧

When the Time of Flood at last replaced
the Time of Drought, its winds brought
not rebirth but deluge, not cleansing
but torrent, not rejoicing but retribution.
The Time of Lamentation arrived as prophesied.
From its shadow the Time of Tentative
Faith, the Time of Renewed Privilege,
the Time of False Glory, of course the Time
of Willful Blindness. Followed by the Time
of Fire's Return, the Time of Final Reckoning.
Beyond the Time of Profound and Lasting
Darkness, however, no record remains.

The Great Egret, never seen here before,
raised black talon from the water, then stopped.
Profile of beak, sepulchral white of the body.
I knew then that you were leaving us,
that the inconsolable reality
had at last arrived. Not that the beast
had come for you, nothing so grand or absurd,
but to announce. The clear and merciless
eye never wavered. Too close, the bird circled,
settled again into its message. Oh wretched
harbinger, what would you have me do?
Within two days, precious one, you were gone.

We didn't want those men here, violating our last
morning hours with their blades and coarse machinery.
Every ash dead from emerald borers, a lost hemlock.
They were efficient in their executions, and I made lives
easy: Just drag the fallen trunks into the woods.
When it was over, I didn't expect you to follow me
to my study. What it cost you, gift to me of our routine.
I got your pillow, resumed my butchery of the language
to define a future I did not want, that I detested.
How much did you realize, dozing beside me
where you belonged, as between phrases I reached
to touch your back, soft fur over bones, that final time?

When your mother lifted you from the pillow
at 6:14 a.m., she knew. I pleaded for one more
selfish day, but the pain … How brave you were.
Those hours, dear god, I won't speak of them.
In afternoon the deer arrived, one young buck
with horns still furred, to announce the end
of our bartered time, the doctor with her trade
of poison for cash. I won't speak of what followed,
each staggering intimacy, garbled whisper.
Courageous, suffering girl. How to fathom all
as it was now. Seventeen days since I lowered you
in my arms, lay you in the hard dark earth.

What if I prefer, Mary, to no longer live in the world?
I held her body to mine, gently, with a love
I knew well my life depended upon. But letting go?
What if I prefer the black shore where my departed
now sleeps forever to the fraught light of salvation?
Look! Canadian geese arrived at our nameless creek.
She had nested on a thread of island. Slender neck
among the wild grasses, partner close by in shallows.
This the spring before the summer that upended us.
Then the morning they were gone. Predator, storm,
or otherwise, what difference? They were gone.
Yes, *that's* the world. Now it was coming for us.

❧

Focus on mammals—abundance of squirrel,
steady migration of deer. Recently at the creek
mink, otter, single inquisitive armadillo,
three young raccoon and parent. At the house
the infamous den of gray fox two years ago,
woodchuck, possum, skunk, fieldmouse, rabbit,
evidence of mole, once an overnight guest
of brown bat on the porch, more rarely coyote
and wild boar. Yesterday bobcat. Lean, exquisite,
taut with attention, methodical between
our blooming crepe myrtle before it leapt
high for prey. A bobcat so near Lucy's grave.

III.

On the back of Judas' human frailty and entrapment,
Jesus made His bones and ascended to myth. Peter, John,
James the Greater—ass kissers and pious wannabes—
singing praise with yes-man Matthew. Andrew, first apostle,
resigned to shadow, Philip and Nathanael the Skeptic
unremarked, Thomas recalled for doubts that branded him.
Simon the Zealot, Thaddeus, rudely named James the Less
rounding out their second tier. Then the whole team gone
excepting John, once His golden boy, now aged and
forgotten in Ephesus, staring over the Aegean to crude calls
of fishermen, that betrayed brotherhood. Only survivor
guilt to sustain him in this bloody, unrepentant narrative.

You never saw an ocean, and after crossing
the border asleep in a blanket-lined shoebox,
never left Tennessee again. From eight weeks old
you lived here with us, from eight weeks
when I carried you in, small in one open hand,
until your death ten weeks short of a 16th birthday.
Here's a photo of the 15th, framed by the window
beyond which, in hydrangeas that have labored
through a flowerless season, I buried you to be
close, where mums, now askew, fade in their vase,
where I've sat talking quietly to you for 45 days.
These are some of the numbers involved.

What physically remains of my father fills a blue
urn on a shelf in my brother's closet, assuming
he hasn't lost, pissed on, or flushed them.
I am youngest, so if the math holds, dying
with me will be the last of the old man's existence.
With final breath, nine decades of anger, desire,
labor, unqualified devotion erased from all time,
all history such to have never existed. Not news,
of course, while musing I watch sky darken,
trees whisper among themselves, the violence
they've threatened, foretold, conjured for days
at last arrive. Why bother to run for shelter?

Danger breathing in the trees, in the darkness.
As often in dream, my legs won't support me
and I struggle, headfirst, on my back, fearful
across wet grass, over foundation stone,
finally onto wooden porch and into the house.
I wake, toss twisted blanket, rise from the couch.
There you are, little one, grinning,
glowing in moonlight, ear restored, eyes cleared,
and it is impossible, this miracle, that you are
returned, yet somehow, my *baby*, and I kneel
to place a hand on your softness. You press your
head into my chest. Then I wake up for real.

Perhaps one of the four, all female, may pause
hovering at salvia or Mexican petunia, but passion's
for hanging feeder. Looping aerial assaults, manic
unequivocal squeaks as each bullies each from nectar
it desires. The sky grays over another week never
to return. Crepe myrtles bloomed out, clematis vines.
In three weeks the hummingbirds will be suddenly
gone on their migration. Where is the male?
Need bother to mention the feeder offers four perches,
each could drink in peace to tiny heart's content?
Lucy gone fifty days. At her grave this morning,
I heard the tanager in the woods but could not see it.

On the 71st morning following Lucy's death, I rise
with the sun and step into our world. At once,
a clicking call long unidentified. From obscured perch,
Crow watches me stop, continue. Mornings cold now,
and I am underdressed but prefer the cold.
Two flickers pinwheeling, their golden underwings
undeniable. The sparkling field. My darkened clogs.
What does it say that I have become a silent creature,
speaking only with the dead—apologies, self-defenses,
gasping clichés? Water frothing over stone,
fluctuating light. All things that exist furious toward
extinction. How it pains me to admit this beauty.

Graybeard driving to town for milk, graybeard
arranging his heirloom pumpkins on the porch.
He's gotten soft, slow, a tad dull in cantation
and augury. Not a fellow to bet on in a knife fight
or pledge fealty to before dawn's field of battle.
In my hand, a curled antler, smooth and cool.
Totem of strength and virility, reads the note,
to shed the old in preparation for what is to come.
The day is lost, yet I find I can't quite let it go.
Some spoken thing, an issue at last determined,
testimony to pure striations of autumn light.
Yesterday would have been Lucy's 16th birthday.

Begin by delineating lower ridge of socket with a press
of fingertip, then continue, intimately, to slight knob
above temple and across the ledge of forehead.
Cheekbone sure beneath cushiony flesh, widening arch
from chin to hinge of jowl. The sure hard final truth.
Don't be distracted by lacrimal from zygomatic,
mandible, maxilla. Nor long tradition of the drinking cup.
Britons of Gough's Cave. Buddhist monks' kapala,
culled from Ganges corpses, abrim with ritual wine.
Lord Byron raising a toast in Shelley's calvaria goblet.
No, just dark sockets keen with blindness, goofy grin
you can't help. *Take me in thy hand! Speak to me, then listen.*

Don was fourth or fifth husband of my mother's
mother, a bulky guy with kinky black hair. I remember
him smiling and laughing easily. He was blind.
I've no idea why he'd married Momo, but I was a kid
so didn't question. They lived in a small house
later razed by the city. In an undated photo, he's wearing
white shirt, tie, cardigan sweater. His loafers shine.
Fallen leaves. Behind, a one-room brick church.
He's grinning, posing, gripping the harness of his Lab
Pepper, of whom I was fond. When Don's time was up,
he was sent packing—Pepper too—with nothing
for what he'd endured. I never saw either of them again.

My parents and brothers, starboard, *Scenic Jungle Cruise*
painted in a flourish along the hull. Photo available
for purchase upon return from the "jungle's" wonders.
I am guessing circa 1960. Of the 60-70 passengers aboard,
every adult and child from bow to stern staring
to the camera. Except, and this is the truth, my parents,
who peer only at each other. Dad in white t-shirt,
Mom a light-colored sleeveless blouse. They are tanned
and beautiful. They are beaming. I, meanwhile, do not
exist here. Look, I realize these indulgences
are of no interest, nor should they be. But oh, those two,
children themselves, all the decades in front of them!

You can't tell if you're code switching or virtue
signifying, but a new speech is required. Like autumn
speaks to the orchard. Like Crow, relentless in
unheeded warning. Like the grave without a stone.
Like a stone to the skull, shiv to the ribs, Zeno's
arrow finally come home to the martyr's breast.
Like the well-seasoned wound, blood under the bridge.
Like the marrow to bone, broth to bowl, spoon
steaming to lips. Like the curse to the night sky,
the oracle, mute. Like the Gypsy woman, a lifetime
ago, who took one sniff of your new girlfriend
and foretold—quite correctly—she was "pure evil."

A good cold dawn for birding: The old toms,
aka the "Five Generals," in congress in the shadows
of the cedar grove. The kingfisher on noisy patrol,
the mallard couple standing placidly, a glimpse
of green heron. Then I am on the front porch swing
of the empty house, pale early light on my legs,
everyone I love, save one, gone from this life.
FedEx lumbers down the gravel drive. A fat kid
with red hair, all smiles, approaches. When he informs
me I've picked a perfect morning to enjoy nature
and drink coffee, then places an awaited package
at my feet, what choice do I have but to agree?

This late October day, clear and temperate, a gift
of the suicide student yesterday in the library.
Campus is closed. The five toms, recently down
to four, seem dispirited and skittish. Black vultures
have completed their efficient roadside work.
If I asserted each golden leaf on the creek surface
to be a soul adrift in passage, would you forgive?
Forgive too my skepticism at the platitudes crowding
the in-box? That confused young woman, her family.
My wife returns from the grocer, and these sad
and bounteous hours will continue with a fine dinner,
wine and song, then, by nature, with darkness.

The COVID card: "I am so dreadfully sorry to miss
your wedding, your gender reveal, your graduation,
your open casket. I've so anticipated the reunion,
the trivia night, bachelorette party and holiday potluck.
How selfish it would be of me now to attend
your gallery opening, endanger your book signing,
put your wellness workshop, Wednesday dinner club,
intervention, birthday, bar mitzvah, baptism at risk.
I know, timing couldn't be worse for the retirement,
child's recital, celebration of life. Understand this is
killing me, that I'll be there in spirit. Deepest apologies.
I was so looking forward. Perhaps another time?"

The endless regrets from that day, a chasm. Why
did it not occur earlier to release you from your harness,
worn since the surgery that upended us? You gave
everything to the extra years we prayed for.
Why did I not think sooner? How could I have failed you?
As you lay, panting, at last I loosened the buckle,
slowly, slowly eased the strap from one leg, from the other.
You were free. My hand in all that plush wonder,
softly. The pain you were in and what this last gift
to us cost you. My beautiful girl, with no more
restraints in this world. Why did it take me so long?
Three months ago today. For two hours, you were free.

I had intended to speak of morning's funnel of glistening
seed, titmice first arrived, calling out their shared bounty,
chickadees quick behind. I tire of grief and grievances,
as I'm certain do you, so was to offer the browned, leafless
twine of morning glory, brutalized throughout summer,
announcing November with its first and only bloom—
a shivering blue trumpet of wonder. Then I saw the remains
of the box turtle moved from harm on Monday, fellow
of yellow shell and skeptical eye whom I liked immensely.
Hit for pleasure, no doubt. Now a dripping goo of shard
and entrail to lift to the woods, cover with fistfuls of decay.
Then wiped my hand on the earth, on this day like any other.

Those hundreds of Sundays, celebrations
of romp and glory, rituals of unlikely
rebirth on the blessed land where we had
been led, our congregation of three. Verses,
howling song, sacrament of a good bone
with some meat on it. The church we built
together. Its foundation. Until the final
testament arrived. By decree, today the light
diminished by an hour, each day after
to further recede. Good. May it go dark.
Until that benediction of silence claims us,
I will bear witness. The righteous fun we had!

I was clever enough not to name her, so clever I was soon
stumbling down our drive each December morning,
meowing across the field, fumbling blue plastic bowl
and tin of Friskies shredded salmon or chunky turkey
in gravy. A calico, handsome patterns of orange-black—
Cat was a hottie and knew it. Her sashay, her lively bounce
on white socks of paw. Sometimes she would walk with me.
I shooed her from the house, our feeders, our frail dog,
fed her all through winter. In the spring, she moved in
with our violent, foul-mouthed neighbors. I saw her once,
outside their sinister shack. She shot me an indifferent look,
flipped twice in the gravel, and resumed licking herself.

IV.

The red raindrops adding their kisses to the red
surge of the river. The red dogs, mouths foaming
red, patrolling the red country roads. The red fields,
red silos, red faces leering from windows, red
clouds churning the red sky. The red classroom,
red courthouse, red history, red justice. The red last
laugh, red prayer, red allegiance. All your life
performed in the red. Red patois, red uniform,
red law, red bottle of courage, red bullet in the rifle's
red barrel. Red skin on fire, red death mask staring
back at choices. Too late. The border's closed.
Listen up: The march of our red future, arrived.

Third week of November and still no proper frost,
though rains have left the morning chill, left blue sky
striped by rafts of cloud, wind soughing in petulant
leaves of the white oak. Three wind chimes twirl
their tuneless song. I am threadbare and underdressed
and crave the cold on my skin, this small recklessness.
Autumn light slants lawn and fenceposts. Soon I will dress,
navigate into the congress of men, barter my hours
with much smallish talk. At the blustery creekside,
the female downy, the mallard couple, even the belted
kingfisher, lately much agitated in flight and warning,
crown tousled—all tolerant, almost as if I were welcome.

The acclaimed one-man show of 1914, the following year
ambulance driver in Flanders beginning in April. Impulsive,
prone to depression, by November the mustard gas,
the discharge, the nervous breakdown. By 1919, his crisis
of faith in the work and two hundred paintings destroyed—
few canvases today remain. At this time the fasting begins,
spirit quest to experience those colors "not perceptible
to the physical eye." You know all this, lessons discerned
or dismissed, know I am ardent admirer for as long
as the 35 years of his life. Edward Middleton Manigault
died of starvation on August 31, 1922. Whether his is a
household name depends, then as now, upon the household.

After the many weeks gone, I was back in my own country.
The final flight on time, I made the call we'd arranged.
Something wasn't right. Robin couldn't hear me over the din,
or it was too late, or … I would be returning to a dark house.
That was that. Hours later, I watched my shuttle mate greeted
by wife and terrier at his front door. Then on into the night,
my unlit country lane. As the driver turned into the long drive,
I blinked in disbelief: a mirage of porch light. My breath caught,
and I knew I'd been given a gift I could not repay, and yes,
I was jagged from travel, but as I fumbled the key—barking
furious inside—as I dropped bawling to my knees, Lucy leaping,
yelping, all over me, it was the happiest moment of my life.

Put aside your conceits for the day. Give yourself
to this solitary road, the crunch of weary boots
on gravel, breath almost a growl, the violence
of arguing wind and crow call. On all sides, earth
raucous with bones. Ahead, a shape in black cowl
emerging from woods. A woman. Depending on
the morning, perhaps she recognizes you and smiles,
opens her basket of alms. Or she sees you, scowls,
what she carries none of your concern. Depending,
she may pass without further notice, leave you
to chance. Or perhaps she kisses your cheek, turns
you gently by the wrist, and guides you home.

Pie and dressing at rest on the counter, cranberries
properly spiked with brandy. Soon, I will spear the bird
onto the rotisserie. Tonight a quiet dinner, silent house,
my wife and me. Meanwhile, thirty years ago, my parents
visiting our cramped apartment. Why had they driven hours?
Perhaps to celebrate our new jobs, new lives. We strove
to impress, my crowning idiocy a roasted goose in that excuse
for a kitchen. Just as they arrived, I sliced my hand deep
shucking an oyster. The blood flowed. Jasper, still a kid,
maybe four years old, boundless for hours, his manic
barking sending us up the walls. A comic catastrophe
of a Thanksgiving, after all. What a wonderful day it was.

> Dead men are heavier than broken hearts.
> —Raymond Chandler

Soon now my detective will hit the cruel streets, possible
title *The Dead Have It Easy*, or *Blood Money's Still Green*.
Hard-knuckled syllables of his name percussive as rifle fire.
My own age, worn by decades, smartass who's tough enough.
He'll live alone on instinct, old mutt his stalwart companion.
Not chaste, but resigned to the world, including its cops.
Seldom paid, though folks never stop arriving with their troubles,
bruised beliefs. Of course, it'll be lies upon lies, a *mille-feuille*
of sweet lies. He'll be a fine cook, drink his gin martinis,
speak often of the wisdom of the French. As to gun of choice?
A Hy Hunter .38 S&W Derringer, cushioned in its original
battered box. Same gun, coincidentally, my father willed to me.

No time of miracles, yet a first light snow, first hours
cold enough to make the body believe. Bluebirds,
vibrant, alert, congregated on branch or dipping beaks
into creek water. I've not left the property for five days,
spoken to no one but my wife, the titmice that confront me
for seed, morning and evening Lucy at her grave.
Later, I will drive to inquire if local chickens are laying,
stop again to fill our bottles with cream-topped milk,
then resume the season's solitude. Only yesterday, I sautéed
a fat turkey liver in butter, ate it sliced rare and salted
in a pool of curdled blood. No sacrament, it was delicious.
Thanksgiving was over. For that too I was thankful.

He is coming to steal my eyes. To seal my mouth
with dirt.[1] And like a bird I sing my hallelujah into the air.
My song belongs to no one.[2] Better than any argument
is to rise at dawn and pick dew-wet berries in a cup.[3]
I have lost the consolation of faith, though not the ambition
to worship.[4] They will offer light to one who is blind.[5]
Illness, madness and death were the black angels that stood
by my cradle.[6] We couldn't imagine another way to live.[7]
Impossible is temporary. Impossible is nothing.[8] But as
the rain enters the soil, river enters the sea, so tears run
to a predestined end.[9] I miss you, in a quite simple
desperate human way.[10] To say goodbye is to die a little.[11]

1   Cormac McCarthy
2   Clarice Lispector
3   Wendell Berry
4   Forrest Gander
5   Leonardo da Vinci
6   Edvard Munch
7   Umberto Eco
8   Muhammad Ali
9   *The Wolf Man* (1941)
10 Vita Sackville-West (letter to Virginia Woolf, Jan. 21, 1926)
11 Raymond Chandler

When the death angel comes, let it be on a winter
morning, cold and clear and still, the bare arms
of birches raised in crooked reverence to the sky.
Let the kingfisher, swift and low over the unbroken
mirror of the creek, call out arrival of his brethren.
If any still exist to note your absence, let them
know that nothing remains to mourn or cherish,
nothing to praise or regret, no majesty in the passing.
Just the great muscled wings closing over you
in embrace, returning you to that abiding dark
of your beginning whence you will not return.
Let it be on a fair winter morning, identical to this.

❧

Twelve drunken drummers drummed out of town;
eleven pipers wheezing through tubercular lungs;
ten leaping lords, arthritic, lame for their holy season;
nine ladies dancing, touching each other discreetly;
eight disgraced maidens no longer a-milking;
seven domestic swans slaughtered by the gamesman;
six organic geese, humanely raised, sold for ransom;
five tarnished rings of betrayal; four rumored calling
birds, extinct; three fat French hens spatchcocked
for the fire; two turtle dove breasts wrapped in
peppered bacon; a partridge poached lightly in brandy
and pear. These, my true love did truly give to me.

Last paragraphs, regarding the death of Wolf 8,
get too blurry to read. Veneration of adopted son
Wolf 21, argued by some as the greatest wolf
who ever lived, Wolf 8 the only male to whom he
deferred. I try again, finish the book, stare out across
a gray winter morning. Fine story, but perhaps
other factors at play regarding those blurry pages?
At the creek, I sit silently for a long while. Intended
some banter with the dead, to speak names aloud
to the sky. But rain hammered hard all night.
Now the frothing water, furious voice overwhelming
my own. No need to question what it signifies.

The square marker of Eliott Nelson "Eli" Horton, Nov. 5, 2009–
May 7, 2010. *There is no other in the world. Mine was the only one.*
Or the following year, a simple black cross for Braxton
Cole Bowman, Nov. 29, 2010—tear away obscuring grass—
Feb. 4, 2011. *Our Sweet Boy.* See slant stone of "Edith Viola Bain,
Mar. 15, 1871-May 30, 1901. Wife of I.L. Morton." Beside,
a mottled arch of thin and fading limestone, "Edith Viola,
May 24, 1901-July 2, 1902. Dau of Mr. and Mrs. I.L. Morton."
To wit: Wife dead at age 30, six days after childbirth. Daughter
13 months later. Of Morton's remains, we've no indication.
Visit Milton Cemetery in the dusk of afternoon, in fresh snow,
or anytime sky spits rain at the dark hills. A favor to yourself.

&

Come not between the dragon and his wrath.

My flat-footed Romeo, blind in her sun, long dismissed,
and my Hamlet, I now realize, played to exhaustion. Must I
always like a whore unpack the heart with words? Bury
the damned father. So I arrive late to the joys of my Macbeth—
arrogant, heedless, barking mutual destruction. Blood will
have blood, and, brother, it won't just be mine. A limited
engagement, as that violence informs neatly my unhinged Lear,
seething in dementia, one boot already stamping the boards.
Who can tell me who I am? You think me madman, fool?
Baby, I'll bring the terrors of the earth. To finish it, Prospero,
emerging from the refuge of my library into Hell's tempest.
Watch the magic. This thing of darkness I acknowledge mine.

The muscled haunches of six Huskies, our good team.
Bruisers Tank and Ulf in the rear, the slender girl
with the brains—Keesha—up front. Boots on boards,
gloves cupping bar. Leaning into turns, tapping claw
brake to slow the beasts from tipping you. And it *is* just you
lunatics, two sleds marking fields in fast straight runs,
carving through pine cathedrals bowed in white.
Icicles in beard, clouds of breath and praise, in deeper
passes stepping off to mush with the pack, pull your weight.
Eyelashes frozen, legs trembling and heart and snot
and even your goddamn eyeballs cold, and the dogs
running, running. Just five years ago, you could do this.

Outside fogged windows, midday
-20 Celsius plus sadistic wind. Inside,
dark elixir rich with beef and cognac.
The crock bowl too hot from the broiler
except for fingertips. You lower face
into a steam of pepper and nutmeg, sweet
paprika. Attack a spongy baguette
slice, slick translucent rings of onion,
dribble of broth, stringy gruyere mess
out of control toward lips. *Trop chaud,*
trop chaud, trop chaud! An hour before—
scarves, boots, numbness, icing tears.

Parading the streets of old Quebec City, every cobbled,
festive corner, canines in winter fineries of vest,
cape and cowl, leggings, leather booties in defense of ice.
Haughty purebred and straining mongrel; whimpering
pup; limping, joint-swollen ancient still in the game.
Toys in blanketed papooses—a quick blink into shocking
cold reality. Flown home today to this silent house,
colored lights on the mirror, glittering boxes on the sill,
nutcracker at blank attention, one rough-hewn wiseman
listing on crooked leg. The unfinished rawhide treat
you left behind. As to those adored animals, alive
in that foreign city, what do any of them mean to me?

This year that broke us, finished. The next, beyond
my reckoning. You left us five months ago today.
I can't continue to be consumed by those last hours,
last minutes, and resolve to try. I open the album
of our beginning. There you are—furball in my palm,
floppy-eared, pink-bellied, runt of the rescued litter!
As those seasons pass, you grow into your beauty,
intelligence, wit and humor. You become Lucy.
There, last image, blur of joy in snow—boundless,
fully arrived. Beyond that final page, all those
lucky years we wanted to have together. And did.
Goodbye, baby. God, you were loved. Rest now.

ACKNOWLEDGMENTS

Asheville Poetry Review: "My flat-footed Romeo, blind in her sun, long dismissed,"; "Soon now my detective will hit the cruel streets, possible"

Blueline: "The muscled haunches of six Huskies, our good team."; "Outside fogged windows, midday"

Cloudbank: "This year that broke us, finished. The next, beyond"

Front Range Review: "The bagworm suspended in cocoon of twigs,"; "I searched back and forth through the pages,"; "My old dog naps at my feet, wheezing quietly,"; "On this day, July 11th, Aaron Burr slayed"

I-70 Review: "Blue grosbeak pecking at parched grass"; "The costly tomatoes and peppers, onions and garlic"

Laurel Review: "On the 71st morning following Lucy's death, I rise"

Porchlight: A Journal of Southern Literature: "The acclaimed one-man show of 1914, the following year"; "Focus on mammals, abundance of squirrel,"; "I am Aries, my wife Libra, so when the horoscope"; "No more of this softness, this kowtowing"; "No more reprieve,"; "Third week of November and still no proper frost,"; "Twelve filth-streaked eggs, never born,"; "We submitted to the sovereignty of our chaos."; "When your mother lifted you from the pillow"

Sugar House Review: "We soaked our sandals when crossing the Rubicon."; "When the Time of Flood at last replaced"

Tampa Review: "I have deadheaded the season's final lilies,"; "Then I am home, Lucy alive, I'm loving on her,"

*

"Pie and dressing at rest on the counter, cranberries" appeared in the Fall 2025 issue of *Gravy*, the magazine of the Southern Foodways Alliance.

ABOUT THE AUTHOR

The most recent of Gaylord Brewer's eighteen books of poetry, fiction, creative nonfiction, criticism, and cookery is the essay collection *Before the Storm Takes It Away* (Red Hen, 2024). His poems have appeared in *Best American Poetry* and *The Bedford Introduction to Literature*. His many international residencies include Hawthornden Castle (Scotland) and the Global Arts Village (India), and he has taught in Russia, Kenya, England, and the Czech Republic. Brewer was awarded a Tennessee Arts Commission Fellowship in 2009. He is a native of Louisville, Kentucky, earned a Ph.D. from Ohio State University, and has been a professor at Middle Tennessee State University for more than three decades.

www.ingramcontent.com/pod-product-compliance
Lightning Source LLC
Chambersburg PA
CBHW030501130626
46549CB00007B/2817